The Popcorn Surprise

Eliza Robbins

NEIGHBORHOOD READERS

Rosen Classroom Books & Materials™

New York

Rob, Matt, and Karen were playing outside.
Mom came outside.
"Let's go for a walk," said Mom.
"Yes, let's go," said Rob.
"Come on, Matt and Karen."

Mom and the children walked down the street.
"What sounds do you hear?" asked Mom.
"I hear a horn," said Rob.
"I hear a fire truck going down the street,"
said Matt.

Mom and the children stopped at the park.
"I hear kids playing," said Karen.
"I hear a bird singing," said Rob.
"I hear a dog barking," said Matt.
Mom and the children walked home.

"What sounds can you hear inside?" asked Mom.
"Listen and you may get a surprise!"
Mom went to the kitchen.
The children listened for sounds.

"I hear a song playing on the radio," said Matt.
"I hear the clock ticking," said Rob.
"I hear the phone ringing," said Karen.
"Is that the surprise?"

"Mom, what is the surprise?" asked Matt.
"The surprise is almost ready," said Mom.
"I hear popping sounds coming from the kitchen!"
said Rob.
"I hear popping too!" said Karen.

"I smell something good," said Matt.
"Here comes Mom," said Rob.
"What did you hear?" asked Mom.
"We heard popping sounds," said Karen.

"What made the sound?" asked Mom.
"It's popcorn!" said Matt.
"Now you can eat the surprise," said Mom.
"Thanks, Mom!" said the children.